ANIMAL TEAMWORK

ANTS
WORK TOGETHER

NORA ELLISON

PowerKiDS
press.

New York

Published in 2018 by The Rosen Publishing Group, Inc.
29 East 21st Street, New York, NY 10010

First Edition

Editor: Melissa Raé Shofner
Book Design: Michael J. Flynn

Photo Credits: Cover Noppharat4569/Shutterstock.com; p. 5 frank60/Shutterstock.com; p. 6 (bee) Bildagentur Zoonar GmbH/Shutterstock.com; p. 6 (wasp) mattckaiser/Shutterstock.com; p. 7 Sanimfocus/Shutterstock.com; pp. 8, 9 Henrik Larsson/Shutterstock.com; p. 10 Kunthanon Surathvirakool/Shutterstock.com; p. 11 nuttapol Phetcharat/Shutterstock.com; p. 13 Pavel Krasensky/Shutterstock.com; p. 14 Manfred Ruckszio/Shutterstock.com; p. 15 De Agostini Picture Library/Getty Images; p. 17 Piotr Naskrecki/Minden Pictures/Getty Images; pp. 18–19 Hiroya Minakuchi/Minden Pictures/Getty Images; p. 20 Patrick K. Campbell/Shutterstock.com; p. 21 Mark Moffett/Minden Pictures/Getty Images; p. 22 AG-PHOTOS/Shutterstock.com.

Cataloging-in-Publication Data

Names: Ellison, Nora.
Title: Ants work together / Nora Ellison.
Description: New York : PowerKids Press, 2018. | Series: Animal teamwork | Includes index.
Identifiers: ISBN 9781508155546 (pbk.) | ISBN 9781508155485 (library bound) | ISBN 9781508155362 (6 pack)
Subjects: LCSH: Ants–Juvenile literature.
Classification: LCC QL568.F7 E45 2018 | DDC 595.79'6–dc23

Manufactured in the United States of America

CPSIA Compliance Information: Batch #BS17PK: For Further Information contact Rosen Publishing, New York, New York at 1-800-237-9932

CONTENTS

MASTERS OF TEAMWORK 4

TINY INSECTS 6

TYPES OF ANTS 8

AN ANT'S LIFE 12

THE COLONY 14

WORKING TOGETHER 16

SEARCHING FOR FOOD 18

STRENGTH IN NUMBERS 20

PROTECTING THE COLONY 22

GLOSSARY 23

INDEX 24

WEBSITES 24

MASTERS OF TEAMWORK

Ants live nearly everywhere on Earth. You've probably seen them marching through your kitchen, across the sidewalk, or up a tree. These tiny creatures are always on the move.

Don't let their small size fool you, though. Ants can do amazing things. This is because they work well as a team. Ants live in huge groups—sometimes with members in the millions—and each ant has a special job. By working together, ants are able to feed, house, and **protect** their giant families.

CRITTER COOPERATION

Scientists believe there are more than 10 quadrillion ants on Earth. That's 10,000,000,000,000,000 ants! In comparison, there are around 7 billion (7,000,000,000) people on the planet as of 2017.

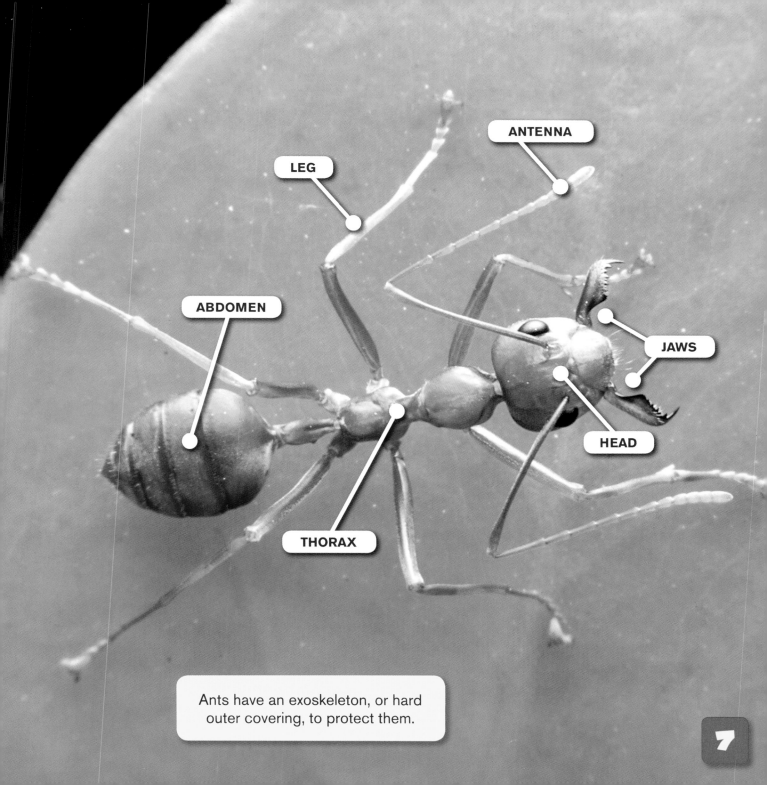

ANTENNA

LEG

ABDOMEN

JAWS

THORAX

HEAD

Ants have an exoskeleton, or hard outer covering, to protect them.

TYPES OF ANTS

A family of ants is called a colony. An ant colony may have millions of members, including workers, drones, and a queen. The queen is the largest ant in the colony, and she only has one job: to lay eggs. A queen ant may lay thousands of eggs each day.

Male ants are called drones. These ants are smaller than the queen, and they have wings. The only job that drones have within the colony is to **mate** with the queen.

CRITTER COOPERATION

Queen ants of some species can live for up to 30 years. However, drone ants don't live very long after mating with the queen.

Queen ants are much larger than worker ants. Some ant colonies will have more than one queen.

Most of the ants within a colony are female workers. Worker ants have several jobs. They protect the queen and keep the colony safe. They're also in charge of finding food for the colony and building the nest the colony lives in. Workers also tend to the queen's eggs and help raise baby ants.

There's a lot to do within a colony, so it's a good thing there are so many workers. Worker ants split up their work, but they also work together. Together, they're very smart.

CRITTER COOPERATION

Ants range in size from about 0.03 to 2 inches (0.08 to 5.1 cm). They're small but strong—they can carry 20 times their own body weight!

Ants are great problem solvers. This moth is too big for one ant to move on its own. However, several ants working together can easily carry it back to the colony.

11

AN ANT'S LIFE

After a queen and drone mate, the queen lays her eggs. Most ant eggs are only about 0.04 inch (0.1 cm) long. They're white and oval shaped. After some time, the eggs hatch into larvae. Larvae look like small worms. They **molt** several times as they outgrow their skin.

When larvae are big enough, they enter the pupa stage. Ants of some species spin a cocoon around their body. During this time, the pupae change into their adult ant form. Most will become workers. Some will become drones. An older colony may also produce a new queen.

CRITTER COOPERATION

It takes between 6 and 10 weeks for an ant to go from egg to larva to pupa to adult.

A colony can't survive for long without a queen since workers can't mate. A colony will only last a few months after a queen dies.

THE COLONY

Ant colonies live inside nests. Many nests are built underground, but some may be built inside plants or up in trees. In underground nests, workers dig tunnels and rooms. The rooms in a nest have different uses, just as the ants have different jobs.

Worker ants put food they collect into special storage rooms. The queen has her own room in which she lays eggs. The eggs are cared for in another room by worker ants. Some kinds of ants even have a room where they keep trash. Ants keep their nest very clean.

CRITTER COOPERATION

Scientists believe some ant colonies are more than 800 years old.

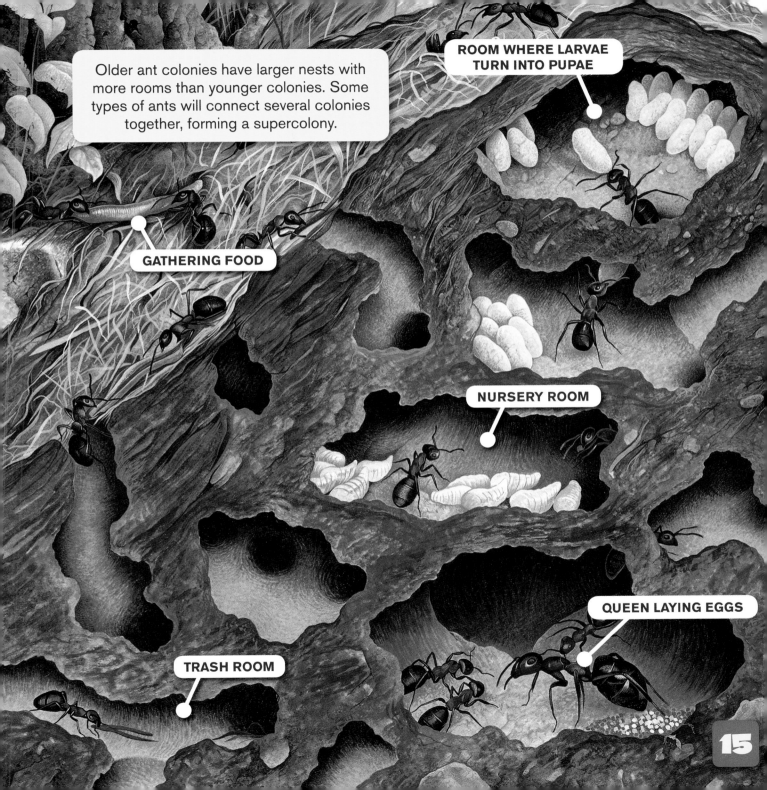

WORKING TOGETHER

Ants can't see well, so they use their antennae to touch and smell each other. This is how they **communicate**. Each colony has its own smell that lets members recognize each other and know when an outsider is present. Ants also produce scent **chemicals** called pheromones. They use pheromones to communicate and create trails for other ants to follow.

Ant colonies are orderly societies in which all members work to keep the colony running smoothly. Some colonies work together so well that they act like a single being, which is called a superorganism.

CRITTER COOPERATION

Ants will often move together as a group. If they reach an obstacle, or something in their way, they'll regroup into a better **formation**.

Ants work together to move heavy objects. Sometimes there's an ant that directs the others where to go.

SEARCHING FOR FOOD

Worker ants are in charge of collecting food to feed their colony. This means feeding anywhere from less than a hundred to several million ants. Luckily, ants know how to work together to get the job done.

CRITTER COOPERATION

Some ants use their strong jaws to **squeeze** liquid from their food. They drink the liquid and get rid of the solid leftovers.

Ants may travel up to 700 feet (213.4 m) from their nest when searching for food. They use pheromone trails to help them find their way back. The trails also let other ants find the food. Some ants leave pheromone trails everywhere they go so they don't travel to the same place twice.

Leafcutter ants cut up leaves with their jaws and carry the pieces back to their nest. The ants don't eat the leaves, though. A **fungus** grows on the leaves as they decay, or break down. The ants eat the fungus!

STRENGTH IN NUMBERS

Army ants are known for their hunting style. They move in groups called swarms and kill any insects or small animals that get in their way. There may be thousands of ants in a swarm. Army ants tear apart their **prey** using their strong jaws.

Army ants live in huge colonies. In order to find enough food, they're always on the move. They'll march together in straight lines or in fan-shaped waves. Worker ants called soldiers have extra-large jaws and protect the other ants as they march.

SOLDIER

CRITTER COOPERATION

Some species of ants will attack nearby colonies and steal eggs and larvae. Many of the stolen young become slaves that are put to work finding food for their new colony.

Since army ants are always moving around, they sometimes use their own bodies to form a bivouac, or **temporary** nest, to protect their queen.

PROTECTING THE COLONY

Scientists have named more than 12,500 species of ants, but they think there might be about 10,000 more. Most ant species work among themselves to keep their own colony safe, well fed, and populated.

If ants from one colony approach those of another, a war may break out between the two groups. Ants will fight to the death to protect their colony. However, there are more than 200 species of fungi-growing ants, and some of that kind of ant species work together and get along.

GLOSSARY

chemical: Matter that can be mixed with other matter to cause changes.

communicate: To share knowledge or feelings.

formation: Shape.

fungus: A living thing that is like a plant, but that doesn't have leaves, flowers, or green color, or make its own food.

jaw: One of the two hard parts on either side of an ant's mouth.

mate: To come together to make babies.

molt: To shed hair, feathers, shell, horns, or skin.

prey: An animal hunted by other animals for food.

protect: To keep safe.

related: Belonging to the same group or family because of shared qualities.

squeeze: To press together closely.

temporary: Lasting for a short amount of time.

INDEX

A
abdomen, 6, 7
antennae, 6, 7, 16
army ants, 5, 20, 21

B
bees, 6
bivouac, 21

C
colony, 8, 9, 10, 12, 13, 14,
        15, 16, 18, 20, 22

D
drone, 8, 12

E
eggs, 8, 10, 12, 14, 15, 20
exoskeleton, 7

H
head, 6, 7

I
insect, 6, 20

J
jaws, 6, 7, 18, 19, 20

L
larva, 12, 15, 20
leafcutter ants, 19
legs, 6, 7

N
nest, 10, 14, 15, 19, 21

P
pheromones, 16, 19
pupa, 12, 15

Q
queen, 8, 9, 10, 12, 13, 14,
        15, 21

S
soldier, 20
stinger, 6
stomach, 6
supercolony, 15
superorganism, 16
swarm, 20

T
thorax, 6, 7

W
wasps, 6
wings, 6, 8
worker, 8, 9, 10, 12, 13, 14,
        18, 20

WEBSITES

Due to the changing nature of Internet links, PowerKids Press has developed an online list of websites related to the subject of this book. This site is updated regularly. Please use this link to access the list: www.powerkidslinks.com/atw/ants